The Believer's Marriage with Christ
by Michael Harrison
with chapters by C. Matthew McMahon

Copyright Information

The Believer's Marriage with Christ, by Michael Harrison,
with chapters by C. Matthew McMahon, Ph.D., Th.D.
Edited by Therese B. McMahon

© 2020 by Puritan Publications and A Puritan's Mind

Published by Puritan Publications
A Ministry of A Puritan's Mind in Crossville, TN
www.apuritansmind.com
www.puritanpublications.com
www.puritanshop.com

All rights reserved. No part of this publication may be reproduced, stored in a retrieval system or transmitted in any form by any means, electronic, mechanical, photocopy, recording or otherwise, without the prior permission of the publisher, except as provided by USA copyright law.

First Electronic Edition, 2020
First Modern Print Edition, 2020
Manufactured in the United States of America

eISBN: 978-1-62663-380-3
ISBN: 978-1-62663-381-0

Table of Contents

Freely Offering Christ to Sinners 4

Meet Michael Harrison 11

Preface 17

The Author's Advertisement to the Reader 22

PART 1: The Text Opened 23

PART 2: The Doctrine 29

PART 3: Application 56

The Postscript to the Reader 75

Other Helpful Works Published by Puritan Publications 77

Freely Offering Christ to Sinners
by C. Matthew McMahon, Ph.D. Th.D.

What is God's will? This question is theologically *daunting*. Where shall we begin to answer it? It depends on the question, or really, the question's *context*. And in this question is a variety of theological concepts which we often take for granted. Does God will, in any way, goodness, blessing or love to the seed of the serpent, with the desire of making those who receive his blessings, loving-kindness, or goodness, *happy* as a result? This is a far different question as it relates to God's *intention* when the free-offer of the Gospel is given to them and falls on their ears by the preaching of ministers. Is there such a thing as a free "offer" of the Gospel if God wills all things, even the election and reprobation of men? If God wills all things, and wills some men to heaven, and others to hell, how can the free-offer *be an offer?* Is God actually *sincere* in it? What does God will in the Gospel call? How does the will of God in the Gospel call extend to the elect and reprobate, and what are his desires and intentions towards either of them? What one believes on those kinds of questions will color *all* of their theology, and how the preaching of the Gospel occurs in their church, or if it does not.

There are a multitude of difficult Scripture passages relevant to the will of God in this way such as Romans 2:4, 9:1ff, Ephesians 1:3ff, Matthew 5:45, Luke 6:35-36, John 3:16, Ezekiel 18:23, and Ezekiel 33:11.[1] There are many Scriptures often used to demonstrate that the Lord is *good to all men in a general way*, but does he desire their salvation *in a real way* if he has reprobated them? Psalm 145:9, Acts 14, and Acts 17 are used to demonstrate this idea in a practical application of the offer. This is even what we hear when people say "common grace," which is defined as that general benevolence given to all men as a result of God's general kindness and love to all men. It seems, that because God is *naturally* good in his nature, he cannot *help* to show his goodness to all men generally. This goodness is specially seen in the *free offer of the Gospel*.

A strict, modern day definition of the "free offer of the Gospel" teaches that God *sincerely* desires the salvation of all men in the preaching of the Gospel, though God does not necessarily grant saving faith to all

---

[1] See my work *The Two Wills of God Made Easy*.

men. This idea ties in to the way Christians understand *God's will.*

The 1647 Westminster Confession of Faith has been the link to the past to the term "offer" for the proposal of the free offer to sinners. Just read any of the puritans in their sermons and preaching and one can see why the Confession uses this term "offer." In Chapter 6 of the confession, Section 3, it says, "Man, by his fall, having made himself incapable of life by that covenant, the Lord was pleased to make a second, commonly called the covenant of grace; wherein *he freely offereth unto sinners life and salvation by Jesus Christ;* requiring of them faith in him, that they may be saved, and promising to give unto all those that are ordained unto eternal life his Holy Spirit, to make them willing, and able to believe."[2] Here we find the word "offer." The Latin word they used here, "offero" means "to bring forward, place before, present, or expose." It is a publication of the Gospel, but it does not mean giving or holding out the *actual effectual call of the Gospel.* That is why the Confession uses the phrase as they do so *freely.*

---

[2] Galatians 3:21; Romans 3:20-21, 8:3; Genesis 3:15; see Isaiah 42:6; John 3:16; Romans 10:6, 9; Revelation 22:17; Acts 13:48; Ezekiel 36:26-27; John 6:37, 44-45; 1 Corinthians 12:3.

In like manner, the Synod of Dordt practically applies this in 5:14 where they say, "And as it has pleased God, by the preaching of the gospel, to begin this work of grace in us, so He preserves, continues, and perfects it by the hearing and reading of His Word, by meditation thereon, and by the exhortations, threatenings, and promises thereof, and by the use of the sacraments." However, historically, in *a puritan's mind*, as it should be in the Christian's mind, the outward preaching of the Gospel is not the same thing as the inward work of grace – they are separate! They are bound by hermeneutical rules, which reside in context of the discussion. There is an outward call that all hear who are present, and there is the inward call that the redeemed of Christ will hear as they are regenerated by the Spirit and believe the Gospel offer by faith alone.

I bring this up, because Harrison is going to offer the Gospel to you, reader. And in this offer, as it stands related to the preaching of the word, the outward indiscriminate preaching of the work of the ministry, God offers Christ to *poor* sinners, (not merely sinners) that they may find rest. Sometimes, when people who like Reformed literature read the puritans, when they use "offere" or "offer" of the Gospel, or they use the phrase, "accept of Christ freely" as he is "offered in the Gospel" readers become somewhat antsy. They wiggle a bit in their seat because in such preaching of Gospel messages, these puritans seem to start a journey to come closer to present day Socinian, Arminian or Semi-Pelagian preachers (even downright Pelagian preachers), who preach that God loves everyone, and desires, *sincerely, the salvation of all men, without discrimination.* But there is no need for such readers to wiggle in their seat at all. Just because the Arminian view of evangelical preaching today uses a very different idea of phrases like "accept Christ" because (in their mind) "God loves everyone" and he is "pleading for you to come to him" which is left up according to your "free will", that *does not mean* that a Gospel offer as in the case of Mr. Harrison's work, is of the same erroneous nature. In fact, Harrison will argue against even *listening* to preachers who preach that way. He would much rather have you, reader, under a faithful ministry and not one of a charlatan.

In this expanded work from a sermon that Harrison gave to his church, he expounds Matthew 22:2-14, "The kingdom of heaven is like unto a certain king, which made a marriage for his son..." He divides the teaching, as all good puritan *preachers* were accustomed to do, into three sections. He first explains the text, then provides the doctrine of the text, and then applies the text. (How I wish preachers would do this today!) His main doctrine, which he faithfully develops is that God in and by the Gospel freely offers Jesus Christ, with all the benefits of his death, to all that are *willing* to come to him and receive him on Gospel-terms.

Harrison is particularly involved in offering the Gospel to those of his congregation that did not, or have not, come to Jesus Christ, as well as those who have come to Christ, but needed a greater assurance that Christ had actually saved them, that they were truly converted. His application of the offer of the Gospel to sinners is astoundingly precise, and with great depth, sprinkled heartily with pastoral concern. God freely offers Jesus Christ to all that are *willing* to come to him, and there is a fivefold *use* of this truth: by way of I. Information. II. Examination. III. Exhortation. IV. Direction. V. Consolation.

As much as this is a plea to sinners on behalf of Jesus Christ, ministers of the Gospel today, even those of the reformed flavor, would do well to listen to Harrison, and learn of him in his presentation. If more preachers would follow his biblical doctrine contained in this work, as well as his style and fervor, I believe there would be more Christians *made* by God's grace, and for Christ's glory, for God looks kindly on such preaching and gives it success, prospering it for his glory, without which, it will not return to him void.

In the grace of Christ,
C. Matthew McMahon, Ph.D., Th.D.
From my study, September, 2020.

Meet Michael Harrison
By C. Matthew McMahon, Ph.D., Th.D.

There is no full biography of Rev. Michael Harrison (1640-1729). What we know of him comes from fragments in works by Edmund Calamy, Thomas Coleman and other writers making mention of him in conjunction with historic information on Edmund Calamy. He was born around 1640 and appears to have been part of the Bard family of Caversfield, (possibly through marriage). We do not have a record of his early years, or his schooling.

We do find the labors of Rev. Harrison mentioned in a church in the parish Church of Caversfield, Bucks. He preached regularly there and resided in the vicarage. Coleman says of him that he "performed the duties of a faithful minister of Christ for a number of years." Harrison became dissatisfied with the terms of conformity. Instead, he maintained familiar connection with evangelical *dissenters*, and finally became fully prepared to recede from the Church of England.

Dr. Edmund Calamy, who was then studying at Oxford, says, "There were at this time monthly fasts appointed by authority, and generally observed very regularly, to implore the divine blessing in order to the success of our forces. At one of these fasts I was at Bicester, and assisted old Mr. Cornish, who was indisposed, at his Meeting House, in the morning; and afterwards walked over to Caversfield, about a mile distant, the Dissenters in a body bearing me company. There I preached in the public Church in the afternoon, and had a crowded Church from the country round. Mr. Michael Harrison preached in the Church, of which Mr. Beard was patron; and he lived in the house adjoining. But Mr. Harrison was now away from home, in Northamptonshire, where he was gathering a congregation of Dissenters about Potterspury, designing to quit the Church and settle among them."

  Harrison's efforts were successful; he soon gathered around him some friends, removed to reside among them, formed a Congregational Church, and purchased a property, on which he fitted up a place of worship. He was the Minster at Caversfield Parish on the Buckinghamshire/Oxfordshire border up to 1690.

  When Harrison moved to Pury, a Mr. John Warr, who formerly lived in the neighborhood of Caversfield, came with him to enjoy the benefit of his ministry. And connected with this circumstance is another, which will show something of the spirit of the times. Coleman makes note, "When Mr. Harrison came to Pury, he brought a pulpit with him, which he deemed it necessary to conceal; therefore, to prevent it being known, Mr. Warr, being a shoemaker, contrived to fill it with shoe-pegs, and brought it among his own goods in a wagon from Bicester."

Harrison's wife owned some property and Harrison used the proceeds of that sale to enable them to purchase the premises on which his dwelling-house and the Church Meeting House were built. When the barn which formed the *humble Meeting House* was prepared, at the request of the people, Dr. Calamy preached at the opening, with a large crowd. In making this move, Harrison trusted in the God who provides, and his faithfulness to bring about true reform to the people of the area for the glory of Christ. Calamy noted in his, "History of His Own Time," that Harrison was a minister of this congregation initially in the Church of England, but later succeeded to the Presbyterian Church.

Harrison labored in this newly established non-conformist church in Potterspury until 1709, for about nineteen years. Afterwards, Harrison moved and became the minister of a Church at St. Ives (a puritan stronghold), in the county of Huntingdon. There too he labored for many years, and died in January, 1726.

His only known works are:
1. *Christ's Righteousness Imputed*, or *the Glorious Doctrine of Free Justification by the Imputation of the Pure and Spotless Righteousness of Jesus Christ*, 1690. (Republished by Puritan Publications).
2. *Infant Baptism God's Ordinance*, 1694. (Republished by Puritan Publications).
3. *The Best Match, or, The Believer's Marriage with Christ* , 1690. (This Current Work). Originally printed in London, for Nathanael Ranew, at the king's-arms in St. Paul's church-yard, 1691.
4. *A Gospel Church Described* in its author, names, head, matter, form, and end wherein are various cases concerning the ministry, divination, admission of members, discipline, schism ... / by Michael Harrison in Potters-Pury, 1700.

For further study:

"Memorials of The Independent Churches in Northamptonshire; With Biographical Notices of Their Pastors, and Some Account of the Puritan Ministers Who Laboured in the County," by Thomas Coleman; Calamy's, "An Historical Account of My Own Life, with Some Reflections, Volume 1;" "Poems by Robert Wilde with a Historical and Biographical Pref. and Notes," By John Hunt; "The Western Antiquary, Volume 8," edited by William Henry Kearley Wright.

1 John 5:12, "He that hath the Son, hath life; and he that hath not Son of God, hath not life."

Preface

This heavenly sermon invites souls to come to Christ, that spiritual feast, that *best* of feasts; costly to the provider, free to the comer.

Christ was crucified to make a feast for us; but it crucifies him afresh, that many who are affectionately invited will not come. They will be starved before they will come to this feast. They will be damned before they will come to Christ. Alas, that they should perish when life is so near! But they that do come, find, by blessed experience, that his flesh is meat indeed, and his blood drink indeed.

There is, 1. Calling. 2. Coming. 3. Union. 4. Communion. Calling is twofold, both outward and inward. Outward calling is by the Gospel, and Gospel-ministry. Inward calling is twofold, ineffectual and effectual. The inward ineffectual call leaves the soul in a worse state than it found it. The quenching of the sparks of heaven is the kindling the flames of hell. And they fall deepest into hell that fall backwards into hell. The inward effectual calling, is, when a soul comes to Christ, that is, believing, (John 6:35). This coming (or believing) determines effectual calling, and begins union. This union is the ground of communion, which on the soul's part, is a partaking of all such spiritual good things, as are purchased by the blood of Christ for believers.

There is nothing that the corrupt nature of man is more averse to than Christ, and faith in Christ. There are no quarrels commenced by the world, the flesh, and the devil, against any grace so much as against justifying faith, nor against any ordinance so much as that which faith comes by, which is the sound and plain preaching of the Gospel, (Rom. 10:17). Through self-fulness, and spiritual distempers, it comes to pass that there is no appetite in the soul after Christ; but this spiritual feast is loathed.

By others Christ is respected only as a remote cause of salvation. They will not allow justification by faith in Christ's blood, without the deeds of the law. They will not come to Christ unless they can make him "a present." As if it were not enough to be joint-heirs with Christ, unless they might be joint-purchasers also.

But the word says, "come, for all things are now ready," (*i.e.* in Christ) (Luke 14:17). "Come, without money, and without price," (Isaiah 55:1). Only, *come*.

Question: Is not this presuming? Answer: Nothing is more contrary to presumption than this. For,

1. It is the greatest piece of self-denial. There is no humility like faith. 2. It is taking the Lord at his word.

Objection: This believing is a slight matter. Answer. It is a senseless and a vile objection. And to speak as the truth is, people do but trifle in matters of the soul, until they are effectually humbled and chastised by the spirit of bondage.

It is a great thing for a man with the heart to believe to righteousness. Such a poor creature is made first to know himself to be a very miserable, lost, undone, helpless, sinking, perishing wretch; and so to know himself, as to abhor himself, and so to abhor himself, as to deny himself, and so to deny himself, as to cast himself into the saving arms of an only Savior, which were stretched upon the cross, and are spread wide open in the promises of the Gospel, to embrace any wretched sinner as will fall into them. This is done by divine light and power. The Spirit convinces and the Father draws. Oh, how the soul cries, pants, yearns after Christ! *Oh nothing but Christ! Nothing but Christ!* It can never be satisfied, until it comes into that blessed heart, where the weary are at rest. This breeds repentance and secures obedience. The repentance is evangelical, and the obedience filial.

Preface

The terrors of the law break the heart into hard pieces, the love of Christ melts it, and makes it flow like water. And the soul that has learned Christ to be her righteousness, finds him to be her strength also, (Isaiah 45:24). In a word, Christ is all. He has done all, he has suffered all, and he must have the glory of every part of our salvation. God will have his Son honored.

Sinners, sinners, come to Christ! Know that there is no salvation but by Christ, neither is there any salvation by Christ, but in Christ. "Israel shall be saved in the Lord with an everlasting salvation," (Isaiah 45:17). Let nothing come between the graph and the stock. Grab hold of the foundation of all this. Let the whole weight of your salvation lie on that foundation which God has laid and not man. You are lost and undone, come as such to Christ; come to a Savior as to a Savior; he will receive you joyfully. Will you not come? O! come, confess your sins, and that you are guilty to be inexcusable! Think to yourself, "O Lord, I cannot answer for what I have done, I cannot bear what I have deserved! But I appeal to the blood of Christ. Your justice might be glorified in my eternal destruction, but it could never be satisfied; but the blood of Christ has both glorified and satisfied your justice. O! let Christ's blood go for mine!

O! sprinkle my conscience with the blood of Christ!" Lie in dust and ashes, and cry for the blood of sprinkling.

Oh Lord, revive among us the doctrine of free grace, the work of conversion, the power of religion, and the spirit of brotherly-kindness and charity.

And now may we see the King of kings, and Lord of lords, sitting on a throne high and lifted up, and his train filling the temple! Now let him be exalted and extolled, and be very high! Now let him be great to the ends of the earth. And blessed be the Lord God, the God of Israel, who only does wonderous things. And blessed be his glorious name for ever, and let the whole earth be filled with his glory. Amen, and amen.

The Author's Advertisement to the Reader

The reader is desired to take notice, that the following sermon was preached to a country-congregation, without the least design of ever being made public. But some of the *then hearers* being very earnest for a copy of the author's notes, with leave to print it, the author (who was at first unwilling, having no desire to be seen in print yet) at last condescended to give a copy, leaving it to their choice whether to make it public or not.

The subject is Christ, the very subject of the Gospel. If the Lord please to bless it, to win over any souls to a cordial closure with Christ, though some may quarrel, the author has his end, and God shall have the glory.

PART 1: The Text Opened

The believer's marriage with Christ: or, a sermon on the parable of the marriage of the king's son.

Matthew 22:2-14, "The kingdom of heaven is like unto a certain king, which made a marriage for his son, And sent forth his servants to call them that were bidden to the wedding: and they would not come. Again, he sent forth other servants, saying, Tell them which are bidden, Behold, I have prepared my dinner: my oxen and my fatlings are killed, and all things are ready: come unto the marriage. But they made light of it, and went their ways, one to his farm, another to his merchandise: And the remnant took his servants, and entreated them spitefully, and slew them. But when the king heard thereof, he was wroth: and he sent forth his armies, and destroyed those murderers, and burned up their city. Then saith he to his servants, The wedding is ready, but they which were bidden were not worthy. Go ye therefore into the highways, and as many as ye shall find, bid to the marriage. So those servants went out into the highways, and gathered together all as many as they found, both bad and good: and the wedding was furnished with guests. And when the king came in to see the guests, he saw there a man which had not on a wedding garment: And he saith unto him, Friend, how camest thou in hither not having a wedding garment? And he was speechless. Then said the king to the servants, Bind him hand and foot, and take him away, and cast him into outer darkness; there shall be weeping and gnashing of teeth. For many are called, but few are chosen."

Here is a parable spoken by our dear Lord Jesus Christ himself, and therefore calls for a hearing ear, and an understanding heart in every one here present. And for our better understanding the mind of Christ in it, let us answer five or six questions.

Question 1: What are we to understand by the kingdom of heaven?

Answer: There is a threefold kingdom of heaven. 1. That blessed everlasting life the saints shall live in the next world. Matt. 5:3, "Blessed are the poor in spirit; for theirs is the kingdom of heaven." 2. There's the kingdom of grace, or the divine life in the hearts of the elect; in whose hearts Jesus Christ has set up his spiritual kingdom. Matt. 13:31, "The kingdom of heaven is like unto a grain of mustard-seed." (See also verse 32). This, and the following parable of the leaven, as a learned man observes,[3] signifies the power and divine efficacy of the Gospel, in and on the hearts of the elect, in the day when they are inwardly renewed by the Spirit.

3. The visible church, comprehending both good and bad people, is sometimes called the kingdom of heaven; as in the parable of the draw-net. Matt. 13:47, "The kingdom of heaven is like to a net that was cast into the sea, and gathered of every kind," *i.e.* the visible church, by the ministry of the word, gathers into it, not only such as are truly sanctified, but all that visibly own Jesus Christ. And in this sense, I humbly conceive, this parable of the marriage is to be understood.

"The kingdom of heaven is like unto a king," *etc.* *i.e.* the great God of heaven, in calling men to, and directing them how to attain eternal life. This God does, as kings use to do at marriage-feasts, who having prepared all things ready, send out their servants to invite the guests. So, God has provided a Gospel-banquet, and sends out the ministers of his word to invite men to come to Christ.

---

[3] Pareus in locum.

Part I: The Text Opened

Question 2: Who is this king? Answer: The great God of heaven, who originally contrived the glorious work of salvation, (as appears in Isaiah 42:1-7).[4] These are the Father's words to Christ, calling him forth to undertake the great work of redemption. Had not the Father contrived a way of salvation for lost sinners, our condition would have been forever hopeless. Jesus Christ is the Father's gift. John 3:16, "God so loved the world, that he gave his only begotten Son" to die.

Question 3: Here is a wedding, but who is the bridegroom, the son here spoken of? Answer: The Lord Jesus Christ, the eternal Son of God, who is the churches spiritual Bridegroom; and, as such, often spoken of in holy scripture. Psalm 19:5, "which is as a bridegroom coming out of his chamber," and this text the ancient

---

[4] "Behold my servant, whom I uphold; mine elect, in whom my soul delighteth; I have put my spirit upon him: he shall bring forth judgment to the Gentiles. He shall not cry, nor lift up, nor cause his voice to be heard in the street. A bruised reed shall he not break, and the smoking flax shall he not quench: he shall bring forth judgment unto truth. He shall not fail nor be discouraged, till he have set judgment in the earth: and the isles shall wait for his law. Thus saith God the LORD, he that created the heavens, and stretched them out; he that spread forth the earth, and that which cometh out of it; he that giveth breath unto the people upon it, and spirit to them that walk therein: I the LORD have called thee in righteousness, and will hold thine hand, and will keep thee, and give thee for a covenant of the people, for a light of the Gentiles; To open the blind eyes, to bring out the prisoners from the prison, and them that sit in darkness out of the prison house," (Isa. 42:1-7).

fathers understood of Christ[5], the spiritual Bridegroom of the church;[6] who assumed human nature in the womb of the virgin, there appeared as the churches heavenly Bridegroom in the world, and so he is held out to us in the parable of the ten virgins, (Matt. 25:1-4), as a heavenly husband that comes to consummate a spiritual marriage with his church.

Question 4: But who is the bride? Answer: The church of Christ, and especially the elect. Jer. 3:14, "I am married unto you." Rev. 19:7, "The marriage of the Lamb is come, and his wife (the church) has made herself ready." Oh the honor given to a believer! To be married to Jesus Christ!

Question 5: What is meant by the feast? Answer: That glorious provision God has made for poor undone sinners in Christ, as union and communion with God and Christ; all the benefits purchased by the death of Christ, such as pardon, justification, sanctification, adoption, and the like, these are the heavenly dishes, served up at this Gospel-feast for believers to feed on. And it's very usual in scripture to represent heavenly

---

[5] Rex ille est Deus Pater; sponsus est Filius Dei. Sponsa pauci electi; Nuptiae disponsatio & copulatio Ecclesiae cum Christo. Pareus in loco.

[6] Corpus suum assumptum ex Virgine & ipse tanquam sponsus Ecclesiae toties promissus per Prophetas, &c. Psalterium Paraph.

things by temporal, and particularly by feasting. Isaiah 25:6, "And in this mountain (*i.e.* Sion, the church, and a type of heaven) shall the Lord of hosts make unto all people a feast of fat things, a feast of wines on the lees, of fat things full of marrow, of wines on the lees well refined," *i.e.* in that day that an elect soul is married to Jesus Christ, there is an heavenly banquet in that heart. Rev. 3:20, "Behold, I stand at the door and knock: if any man hear my voice, and open to me, I will come in and sup with him, and he with me."

Question 6: Who are the servants sent out to invite the guests to the wedding? Answer: the servants[7] are God's ministers both of the Old and New testament. The first were patriarchs, then Moses, and the prophets, and last of all the apostles, and their successors. So, I that am now preaching to you, am one of these servants, come to invite you to come to Christ. The Jews, they refused, so now the Gospel is preached to the Gentiles, whose offspring we are.

---

[7] Primi Servi fuerunt Patriarchae: posteriores, Moses & Prophetae. Pareus in loco.

PART 2: The Doctrine

Having in this way explained the parable, we come now to the observation; and though this pregnant text might afford many, yet I shall content myself with only one which comprehends the very heart and marrow of the text.

DOCTRINE: God in and by the Gospel freely offers Jesus Christ, with all the benefits of his death, to all that are willing to come to him and receive him on Gospel-terms.

In speaking to this heavenly truth, I shall endeavor these five things. First, show who it is that makes this offer to sinners, God the Father. Secondly, what is offered, Jesus Christ. Thirdly, in which is Christ offered, *viz.* in the Gospel. Fourthly, to whom does God offer Christ, *viz.* to all that are willing to come to him. Fifthly, what is it to come to, and receive, and accept of Christ.

Question: First, who it is that offers Christ and salvation to sinners? Answer: It is the great God of heaven. John 3:16, "God so loved the world, as to give his only begotten son," to die. Christ indeed is the Redeemer by whom we are saved from wrath to come; it is by him that we have redemption, (Eph. 1).

But this way of salvation was of the Father's contrivance; he calls Christ forth and employs him in the great work of redemption. Isa. 49:5, "And now, saith the Lord that formed me from the womb, to be his servant, to bring Jacob again to him." These are the words of Christ,[8] in which he shows, that the glorious work of redemption, and bringing back the elect to God, was a work to which he was called and fitted by the Father. And therefore, the work of redemption is sometimes attributed to the Father; Col. 1:12-13, "Giving thanks to the Father," *etc.* And you and I should be much in adoring the infinite goodness and free mercy of God that has remembered us in our low estate; because "his mercy endureth for ever," (Psalm 136:23). We were sinking into hell, and eternal perdition. Had not the Father pitied us and contrived our salvation, we would have perished without remedy for ever. Look on that new and living way to the Father by Christ, and see the Father's eternal love in it, (2 Cor. 5:18-19). All things are of God, who has reconciled us to himself by Jesus Christ; and has committed to us the ministry of reconciliation; in other

---

[8] Hoc capite continetur Prophetia de Officio Christi. Piscator.

words, that God was in Christ reconciling the world to himself. O! I implore you adore, admire, and sing the Father's praise for giving you a Christ!

Question: Secondly, what is it God freely offers us? It is the Lord Jesus Christ. And this may be matter of wonderment to men and angels, that God should give us his Son, one who was in the form of God, and thought it "no robbery to be equal with God," (Phil. 2:6). Him who was the brightness[9] of his Father's glory, and the express image[10] of his person, and upholding all things by the word of his power. Him who is "Alpha and Omega, the Beginning and the Ending, which is, and was, and is to come, the almighty," (Rev. 1:8). A Lord of lords, and king of kings, (Rev. 17:14). The image of the invisible God, (Col. 1:15). The only begotten of the Father, (John 1:14). Him in whom all the fulness dwells, (Col. 1:19). Him who is white and ruddy, the chiefest of ten thousand, (Song of Songs 5:10-11). He is "Altogether lovely," (Song of Songs 5:15), a glorious infinitely complete person! Search heaven and earth and none can be found like Christ.

---

[9] This word signifies more than brightness, even such a brightness as has a luster cast on it from some other thing. Sicut Sol radios ex sua substantia gignit; sic Pater ab eterno ex sua substantia Filium genuit. *Critica Sacra.*
[10] Character figura idem.

But to illustrate this greatness of God's love in giving Christ, let us consider by what notions, and in what relations Jesus Christ is held out to us.

1. Jesus Christ is a Redeemer, and, as such, he is offered to us. Isa. 59:20, "The redeemer shall come to Zion." Eph. 1:7, "We have redemption through his blood, the forgiveness of sins." Now Christ's being a Redeemer, intimates two things to us. (1.) That we are by nature in a state of bondage; if it were not so, we should not need a Redeemer. One that is already free, does not need one to make him free. And it is here that the carnal world sets so light by Christ, and all the offers of his grace, because they are not sensible of their bondage and slavery. Now by nature we are slaves to sin, (2 Peter 2:19). They are the servants of corruption, (Titus 3:3), serving diverse lusts and pleasures. And not only so, but we are the devil's slaves, Eph. 2:2, "Wherein in times past ye walked."

Also, (2.) The consideration of Christ as a Redeemer, intimates to us, that there was a price paid to redeem lost man from the slavery of sin and Satan, and this was the blood of Christ the Redeemer. 1 Peter 1:18-19, "Ye were not redeemed with corruptible things, as silver and gold, but with the precious blood of Christ, as of a lamb without blemish, and without spot."

Now Christ is offered to you to be your Redeemer from hell and wrath. But who among you are willing to receive him, to come to him? It may be you will say, "we are all willing to have Christ as our redeemer." No, no, there's none willing but only such as are sensible of their slavery. The poor sinner that finds himself bound with the chains of sin, led by Satan captive at his will, and so ready to drop into hell, O! for a Redeemer for such a poor soul, such a soul will cry and beg for Christ.

2. Christ is a mediator. 1 Tim. 2:5, "There is one mediator between God and man, the man Christ Jesus," and this shows us, that fallen man can have no access to God immediately by himself. There is so great a breach between God and him. Psalm 7:11, "God is angry with the wicked every day." Let a man in an unregenerate estate do what he will, God is *angry* with him. If you are out of Christ, while you eat, sleep, walk, yes, when you pray, God is angry with you. The sacrifice of the wicked is abominable to him. You cannot come near him, for he is a consuming fire. Therefore, we must have a Mediator, a middle person to reconcile an offended God, and a rebellious sinner to take up the quarrel between God

and man. Isaiah 27:5, "Let him take hold of my strength, that he may make peace with me, and he shall make peace with me." There is no way to make peace with God, but by Christ. Eph. 2:14, "He is our peace." Now, who will have Christ as a Mediator? None but those that are sensible of the breach that sin has made between God and their souls.

3. Jesus Christ is a Savior, and as such he is offered to us. Luke 2:10-11, "Behold I bring you good tidings of great joy, which shall be unto all people: for unto you is born a Savior, which is Christ the Lord." Now this supposes we were all by nature lost, otherwise there is no need of a Savior. Matthew 18:11, Jesus Christ came to "seek and to save that which was lost." Sinner, do you see yourself lost? Do you see your need of Christ a Savior? Then a Savior will be welcome. This is sweet news to a poor lost soul that sees he is undone by sin.

4. Jesus Christ is an advocate. 1 John 2:1, "If any man sin, (i.e. any of the elect, and of those that Christ died for, he did not die for all, but only for the elect) we have an Advocate with the Father, Jesus Christ the righteous." And he is not only an advocate, but an

intercessor.[11] Now this supposes, that we were accused to the Father. If we had not been accused, there would have been no need of an advocate or intercessor. We were accused, 1. By Satan, Rev. 12:10, "The accuser of our brethren is cast out;" he accused Job and Joshua the high priest. 2. We are accused by our own consciences, (Heb. 2:14). 3. We are accused by the word of God, so far as we violate any of its precepts, it accuses us. John 5:45-46, "Think not (Christ says) I will accuse you to the Father, there is one that accuseth you, even Moses, in whom ye trust," *i.e.* the scriptures that Moses wrote. 4. The wicked world, they accuse the people of God, cry out against them for their holiness, strictness, heavenliness. 1 Peter 3:16, they "speak evil of you," as evil-doers, and they falsely accuse your good conversation in Christ.

Now Christian, are you sensible of these several accusations? O! then a Christ to speak for you will be exceedingly welcome! Well, here he is tendered to you. If you have felt the cries and accusations of conscience against you, then the tidings of an Advocate will be welcome.

---

[11] "Therefore will I divide him a portion with the great, and he shall divide the spoil with the strong; because he hath poured out his soul unto death: and he was numbered with the transgressors; and he bare the sin of many, and made intercession for the transgressors," (Isa. 53:12).

5. Jesus Christ is a King, and he is Lord, and as such he is offered to us. Rev. 17:14, "King of kings," but particularly he is King of his church. A king is to govern, so, Jesus Christ gives laws to his people, and he will see that his laws are executed. Isaiah 33:22, "The Lord is our law-giver, the Lord is our king, he will save us." And in this Christ has the preeminence above all earthly kings. Their laws and government reach but to the outward man, but the government of Jesus Christ is over hearts. He rules in the souls of his people. Psalm 110:3, "Thy people shall be a willing people in the day of thy power." Sirs, are you willing to be Christ's subjects, to let him rule in your hearts? It is the sweetest government in the world. Matthew 11:28-29, "Come unto me—my yoke is easy, and my burden is light."

But none will come to Christ in this respect, but only they who are sensible of their own unruly passions and carnal affections, that they are in no way able to rule and govern themselves. Which was Paul's case in Romans 7:23, "But I see another law in my members rebelling against the law of my mind, and leading me into captivity to the law of sin and death." And finding it in this way with him, he flies to Christ, who by his kingly power was able to rule and subdue them, verses 24-25, "O wretched man! Who shall deliver me from this body of sin and death? I thank God through Jesus Christ our Lord." And, Romans 8:2, "The law of the Spirit of life in Christ Jesus, hath made me free, from the law of sin and death."

6. Jesus Christ is a priest, and as such offered to us in the Gospel. The high-priest under the law was a type of Christ, as likewise all those offerings and oblations were typical of Christ, and his offering up himself to the Father. Heb. 2:17, "In all things it behoved him to be made like unto his brethren, that he might be a merciful and faithful high priest, in things pertaining to God, that he might make reconciliation for the transgressors." Now who among you are willing to have Jesus Christ as a priest? None but those who see their sin and misery; for the work of Christ as a priest, is to make reconciliation. Oh sinner, do you see sin, and that the breach between God and your soul is so great, that none but Christ can make God and you friends? He must bear your sins, (Isaiah 53:5-6; 2 Cor. 5:21). He himself is the altar, priest, and sacrifice. If this is so, then Christ will be welcome to you.

7. And lastly, Jesus Christ is the spiritual husband and bridegroom of his church; in this way he is held out in this parable. We are not only invited to the marriage of the Son, but we are invited to come and marry with the Son; not only as bride-maids to wait on the Son, but to *be* the spiritual bride, to come and marry with, and lie in the heart of the Son. In this way as the church's spiritual husband, the Lord Jesus Christ is often so spoken of, as in the parable of the ten virgins, (Matthew 25:1). And so Ezekiel 16:8, "Now when I passed by thee, and looked upon thee, behold, thy time was a time of love, and I spread my skirt over thee, and covered thy nakedness; yea, I swear unto thee, and entered into a covenant with thee, and thou becamest mine." So, throughout the book of the Song of Songs, Christ and believers convene in this sweet relation. Christ owns the church for his spouse. Song 2:16, "My beloved is mine, and I am his;" these are the churches words, owning her relation to Christ. And Song 4:8-11, in these four verses the church is called four times *spouse*. Though the world disowns the believer, Jesus Christ owns him. Here's a sweet, a heavenly match, Christ and the believer are married! And this is not a forced match, no, Jesus Christ accepts of sincere souls in

this relation with a glad heart. Song 3:11, "Go forth, O ye daughters of Zion, and behold king Solomon (*i.e.* Christ, of whom Solomon was a type) with the crown wherewith his mother (*i.e.* the church) crowned him in the day of his espousals, (to his elect in a holy, gracious, heavenly union) and in the day of the gladness of his heart.

Now my dear friends, here's an offer for you, a heavenly husband; Oh do not be so unkind and cruel to yourselves, as to deny Christ. I am one of these servants. I have a commission from Christ, yes and from the Father also, to assure you, that if you are willing, Christ is yours. This is my business, the errand I come on, to invite you to come to Christ. Come, all things are ready on Christ's part; he has died, and made his soul an offering for sin. Will you not come, will you be damned rather than part with your sins? O! come, Rev. 22:17, "The Spirit saith, come; and the bride saith, come, whoever will, let him come." But I shall speak further to this, when I come to a use of exhortation.

Thirdly, wherein, or by what means, does God offer Christ to lost souls in the Gospel? The law requires perfect obedience, and curses every one that does not continue in all things to follow Christ's commands. Gal.

3:10, "Cursed is every one that continueth not in all things written in the book of the law to do them." This is terrible news: for where is the person under heaven, that has continued in all things, that has fulfilled the law, and may expect eternal life on law-terms? Whoever kept one commandment of God? No, we have all sinned and come short of the glory of God. So, that by the works of the law (or by our obedience to God's law, or keeping his commandments) "shall no flesh be justified in his sight," (Rom. 3:20). Therefore, we are all by nature under the curse of the law; the law speaks nothing to the sinner but wrath and terror. It brings the sinner to the bar, and there pronounces sentence of condemnation against him, and there leaves him in the hands of justice, to expect the execution of that fearful sentence, "Go ye cursed," (Matthew 25:41). The law gives no ground of hope to a poor sinner to expect salvation. But now the Gospel brings the glad-tidings of a Savior. Luke 2:10, "Behold, I bring you good tidings of great joy, which shall be unto all people: for to you is born a Savior, which is Christ the Lord." As if the angel had said, come, you that are under the curse and fiery sentence of the law, do not despair, the great God has in infinite mercy contrived a way to save you from your sins and fears; there's a Savior born for you, who is able and willing to save to the utmost all those that come unto God by him. This blessed news of a Savior was reserved for Gospel-times in a great measure, (2 Tim. 1:10), for life and immortality are brought to light by the Gospel. And therefore, this is the very business of a Gospel-ministry to preach Christ to men, and to invite people to come to Christ. 2 Cor. 5:20, "We are ambassadors for Christ, we pray you in Christ's stead, be ye reconciled to God." And that great apostle Paul, who had well considered what he was to preach, sums up the whole of his ministerial office in a little compass, 1 Cor. 2:2, "I resolved to know nothing among you, but Christ, and him crucified;" *i.e.* I had no purpose to teach any other doctrine than that which is the most necessary and only saying doctrine, the way of salvation by a crucified Christ. For indeed this is the only saving knowledge, as in that saying,[12] if you know Jesus Christ well, it is enough, though you are ignorant of all other things; but if a man does not know Jesus Christ, all other knowledge will do him no good.

Accursed, then, is that Platonical way of preaching, that cries up virtues, and puts people on legal

---

[12] Si Christum discis, satis est, si caetera nescis: Si Christum nescis nihil est, si caetera discis.

performances, but hides from people the pearl Jesus Christ. O! bless God for the Gospel, and for a Gospel-ministry! And hear those ministers that preach Jesus Christ. Were it not for the Gospel, and a Gospel-ministry, in what would England differ from America?

Question: To whom does God freely offer Christ in the Gospel? Answer: Jesus Christ is not offered to fallen angels, they are in a fearful state, inevitably sentenced to perdition. God could have recovered them if he had pleased. Jesus Christ might have been their Savior, and not ours. They are a nobler order of creatures than we are; but it seemed good to the wisdom of God to pass them by; when they turned their backs on God, he let them go. Heb. 2:16, "For verily he took not on him the nature of angels, (or he took not hold of angels) but the seed of Abraham."

2. The Jews who had the first offers of the Gospel, but refused, are by the all-wise God for the present passed by, he has withdrawn his offers from them, and left them at present to sit in darkness, and in the regions of the shadow of death. There is indeed a time when the blindness shall be plucked from off their hearts, and they turn to the Lord, and they shall be

converted, (See Romans 11 in total, and Zach. 12:10). O! let us beg that God would hasten it.

3. There is an abundance of the Gentile world that yet sits in darkness, and in the regions of the shadow of death, that never yet had the Gospel preached to them. O! what vast countries are there in the east and west indies that never heard of a Savior, that never had any books to read, but the creatures of the sun, moon and stars! These we should pity, and pray for their conversion. It is a dreadful case not to have the Gospel. Lord, send out your light and truth, (Psalm 43:3). There is a day when the fullness of the gentiles shall come in, as may be seen by well considering these scriptures, Isaiah 49:6, and Isa. 61 throughout. This will be then a golden time, when Jews and gentiles shall be converted, and the earth filled with the knowledge of the Lord, as the waters cover the sea. O! beg and pray for such a time, that Jesus Christ may be glorified on earth as he is in heaven.

4. There are an abundance even in the Christian church, that are baptized and called Christians, and make some kind of a profession of religion, that have so often and so long resisted the saving offers of Christ in the Gospel, and trampled on that sweet and blessed

blood of Jesus, that Jesus Christ is done with them. He has "sworn in his wrath that they shall never enter into his rest," (Heb. 3:11). O! it is dreadful for a person to *outstand* his day of grace. Be afraid sinner lest it should be your case; if Jesus Christ should say, "I am done with that swearer, I'm done with this drunkard, with that worldly, proud, scoffing carnal wretch. I've often invited him, warned him, but to no purpose; I'm done with him, he shall never be called anymore for me." These indeed have Christ offered in the word, but the Spirit is gone; God says of these, as once he did of Ephraim; "Ephraim is joined to idols, let him alone." This is a dreadful case! Of such as these the apostle speaks, Heb. 6:4-6, "For it is impossible for those who were once enlightened, and have tasted of the heavenly gift, and were made partakers of the Holy Ghost; and have tasted the good word of God, and the powers of the world to come: if they fall away, to renew them again unto repentance; seeing they crucify to themselves the son of God afresh, and put him to an open shame." This is a hard scripture, and very much stumbles some weak, but upright Christians, therefore I'll anatomize it to you.[13]

---

[13] Locus perobscurus & difficilis, unus haud dubiè ex illis, de quibus Petrus dixit, quaedam esse in Epistolis Paulinis; quae homines indocti & instabiles Pervertant, suo ipsorum exitio.

1. Some, as Novatus and his followers, from this scripture broached his pernicious opinion, that those that sinned after baptism, could not be renewed to repentance. But this opinion is long ago out of doors.

2. Others would here infer the falling away from grace; taking these expressions (to be once enlightened, to taste the heavenly gift, to taste the good word of God, and the powers of the world to come) to intimate a sound work of conversion and regeneration. But that cannot be the sense, because true grace, and the seed of regeneration can never be lost, neither can a person in Christ finally fall away from Christ, as appears from that one text, which I shall now only name among many others to that purpose, 1 Peter 1:23, "Being born again, not of corruptible seed, but of incorruptible, by the word of God which liveth and abideth for ever." And this cannot be better expressed than in the words of that learned and godly divine, Mr. William Pemble in his book, called *Vindiciae Gratiae*. "For the habit of grace in the regenerate, we affirm that it is constant, abiding forever in them, in whom it is once planted; so that he that is once converted, cannot so shake off the grace of his first, as to need a second conversion; and a sinner once raised from death unto Christ, through the infusion

of spiritual life, he dies no more, but lives for ever to the glory of God."

As appears from that of the apostle, 1 Peter 1:2-3, what is this seed by which we are born again? Is it not the word either alone or principally considered, because that is the instrument; no, it is by the power of the Spirit, without which the word is but a dead sound. So then, this seed is the power or virtue of the Holy Spirit. But why is this seed called *incorruptible?* In respect of itself it is so, but it is so described in this place, in respect of the effect it produces *quatenus semen*, it produces fruit like itself, *incorruptible and immortal.* We are not born of corruptible seed, for that perishes, and what is born of it; but of incorruptible, that lives and endures forever. And so, whatever is born of it, is immortal. This quickening power of the Spirit lives forever; not only in itself, but in us also. Therefore, a soul once in Christ by renewing grace, can never finally fall away.

Others say that the apostle speaks here only by way of supposition, if these fall away, it is impossible to renew them, *etc.* But they can never fall away. But, 4. others say, these were but the common workings of the Spirit on the hearts of hypocrites. And these come nearest to the sense; and it must be confessed, hypocrites may go a great way in religion, and have even some taste and relish of the things of God in their spirits, as appears in the stony-ground-hearers, (take heed reader that you are not an hypocrite!) Matt. 13:20, they are said to receive the word with joy, and yet not have any saving grace in their souls. *But,*

5. Others expound this scripture of those extraordinary gifts of the Spirit Christians had in the apostle's days, such as the gift of healing, speaking with tongues, *etc.* These extraordinary gifts were from the Spirit: and no doubt, such as had any of these miraculous gifts were much pleased and delighted with them, and many that had them perished, as may appear from comparing these scriptures, Matthew 7:21-24 and Gal. 3:3-4. And this I humbly conceive to be the sense of this scripture. O! it is dreadful to sin against light, against convictions; to live under a Gospel-ministry, and get no good by it!

But now, these excepted, Jesus Christ is offered to all in the visible church, and all are freely invited to come in, as in the text. Now these free and general offers are seen in these two scriptures, Isaiah 55:1-3, "Lo, every one that thirsteth, come ye to the waters, and he that hath no money; come ye, buy and eat, yea, come, buy wine and milk, without money, and without price," *etc.* And Rev. 22:17, "The Spirit saith, come; and the bride saith, come; and whoever is athirst, and will, let him come, and take of the water of life freely."

But in a peculiar manner, though Jesus Christ is offered in general to all, yet he is particularly offered to such as are wounded, and afflicted in their soul for sin, and these alone are the people that will welcome a Savior. Luke 5:31-32, "The whole need not a physician, but those that are sick;" it is the wounded soul that needs a remedy, the sick soul that needs a physician; the prisoner that needs a Redeemer; the lost sinner that needs a Savior. Now if there is in this congregation any trembling, bleeding, wounded spirits, that are with the jailor crying, "what shall I do to be saved! O! I'd give ten thousand worlds if I had them for a Christ!" *etc.*, to such is the word of this salvation sent. Poor soul! Here is a Christ for you! Be of good cheer, arise, he calls you, hear what he says to you, Matthew 11:28, "Come unto me all ye that labour, and are heavy laden, and I will give you rest."

Thirdly, what is it to come to Christ, to believe in Christ, to receive and accept him on Gospel-terms?

This coming to Christ, it is not a mere dogmatical and opinionative faith, a mere persuasion of the truth of scripture, to believe the articles of your Creed, and profess yourselves Christians. This is very common; but this coming to, and believing in Christ is a saving grace, worked in the hearts of people by the word and Spirit of God, by which being awakened to see their sin and misery, that hell and wrath due to them for sin. They despair in themselves, and all other creatures, and speedily fly from their sins and themselves to Jesus Christ, resting on him alone for justification, pardon and eternal life.

This is coming to Christ; and not a person under heaven, that does not have such a particular faith as is here described, did yet ever come to Christ.

1. You have here its nature, it is a saving grace, *i.e.* not what is common to believers and unbelievers, but peculiar to only believers. There is a common faith, a common love, a common repentance, and common obedience, which hypocrites may have; and there is a special saving faith, a heavenly new-distinguishing work of the Holy Spirit on the heart, which is peculiar to a saint, and none but a saint has it. You have both of these expressed in that one scripture, Heb. 10:39, "We

are not of them which draw back to perdition; but of them which believe to the saving of the soul." Here is, first, common faith. Some that draw back, *i.e.* were unsound, rotten-hearted professors, who had a common faith, enough to make them profess and own Christ in time of peace, but not enough to go through with their profession; and here is a saving faith, a believing to the saving of the soul. O! look to it, that your grace is more than what is common!

2. Here is the necessary preparation to it, and that is, the heart awakened, and humbled, and broken for sin; this brokenness of heart for sin, it is not faith, nor coming to Christ; but it is a necessary preparative to it, an unbroken heart, unhumbled soul will never come to Christ. Luke 5:31-32, "The whole need not a physician, but they that are sick." It is necessity that drives men to Christ, when they see themselves undone, ready to drop into hell. The law curses them, and they are beset on every side. Like those in Acts 2:37, when they were pricked at the heart, then they cried out, "what shall we do to be saved?" Now verse 38 says, that the apostle directs them to Christ; the sinner must first despair in himself, before he will come to Christ.

People cry out against spiritual, lively, searching and quick preaching. But why? O! this drives people to despair. There is two sorts of despair. (1.) To despair of getting to heaven in a state of sin, while a man is unregenerate, unsanctified; and truly such a despair as this we do preach. I tell you from the Lord Jesus Christ, that every one of you living and dying in a Christ-less state, you will be as surely damned, as if you were in hell already. John 3:3, "Except you are born again, you cannot see the kingdom of God." (2.) There is another kind of despair, and that is, when men despair of ever obtaining mercy though they do repent, and leave their sins. We do not preach any such despair as this. But on the contrary, do all we can to draw, and to encourage men to come to Christ with an assurance of pardon. Isa. 55:7, "Let the wicked forsake his way, and the unrighteous man his thoughts; and turn to the Lord, and he will have mercy upon him, and to our God, for he will abundantly pardon."

    3. There is the instrumental cause of this blessed work on the soul, and that is, the word of God. Romans, 10:17, "Faith comes by hearing, and hearing by the word of God." If you would be drawn to Christ, wait on a Gospel-ministry.

4. There is the efficiency of this heavenly work, the blessed and Holy Spirit of God. Eph. 2:8, faith is "the gift of God." The Holy Spirit is called the Spirit of faith, (2 Cor. 4:13), because the Spirit, by the word, can draw a soul to Christ. Therefore, wait on the ministry, but beg, as the church does, for the drawings of the Spirit, Song of Songs 1:4, "Draw me."

5. Here is the *terminus a quo*, or what a man flies from in the day when he in this way comes to Jesus Christ. (1.) He flies from sin. Now, "the wicked forsakes his way, and the unrighteous man his thoughts," (Isaiah 55:7). Now is the time when a man has right apprehensions of the hellish destructive nature of sin; he sees sin now to be worse than plague, famine, sword, or any temporal evils, and therefore flies from it, as Lot did out of Sodom, or the Jews out of Egypt. He hastens now as for his life, to cleanse his hand, and his heart from all pollution, both of flesh and spirit; now sin appears what it is in itself. He flies from heart-sins, secret sins, vain thoughts, as well as open sins, (Psalm 119:113, 139:23).

(2.) He flies from himself. Whatever high thoughts he might have of himself formerly, he now sees himself one of the filthiest and most loathsome creatures under heaven, and this especially in the vileness of his heart and nature, by reason of that fountain of original sin and corruption which is in him. He now sees the plague of his heart, (1 Kings 8:38). And here he now loathes himself, condemns and judges himself in the sight of God, Romans 7:28, "O wretched man that I am! Who shall deliver me from this body of death?"

6. Here is the *terminus ad quem*, that to which the poor awakened sinner flies, and that is, to Jesus Christ. Indeed, faith in general looks to the whole word of God, and believes whatever is revealed in it to be true on the divine authority of the word itself, yielding hearty obedience to every command, trembling at the threatenings, (Isaiah 57:15).[14]

But the principal and special act of saving faith, is a receiving Christ,[15] and a resting on him alone for justification, sanctification, and eternal life. And although this special act of faith, as leaning, resting, hanging upon, and trusting in Christ crucified, is so much exploded in this corrupt age, by men of corrupt

---

[14] ...miser ego homo, infelix ego homo. Montan. Aerumnosus ego homo. Beza. Ah me miserum, quis me liberabit ab hac dira servitude. It signifies one that is wearied with troublesome and continual combats, like as a champion striving a long time, and this is likely a last thing to be overcome; it is the voice of one breathing after deliverance. Calvin.

[15] Receiving Christ is the puritan term which is synonymous with "accepting Christ" in this manner. – Editor.

minds, yet it is, and ever will be, a sweet and heavenly truth, prized by the church of Christ, more than all the world besides, and clearly proved from the holy word of God. John 1:12, "As many as received him, to them gave he power to become the sons of God." Song of Songs 8:5, "Who is this that cometh up from the wilderness, leaning upon her beloved?" So, Eph. 1:13, "In whom also ye trusted, after that ye believed." This leaning, trusting, resting upon Christ, is the proper act of justifying faith, and it has three degrees: adherence, recompence, assurance.

    1. Adherence, which singles out Christ and holds him, and as it were, by the hand of faith, takes him by the hand, for the stay and support of the soul. The poor sinner seeing his own nothingness, he flies to Christ, hangs on him, cleaves to him, looks to him in every strait, when he has nowhere else to look, nor none else to trust to. 2 Chron. 20:12, "We know not what to do, but our eyes are unto thee."

    2. Recompence, which is an acquiescence on Christ, the soul resolves to rest on Christ, let the issue be what it will, as Job 13:15, "Though he slay me, yet will I trust in him." Or as Esther 4:16, "I will go in unto the king, and if I perish, I perish." This is what the believer

says, "I will hang on Christ's skirts, believe in him, follow after him, if I perish, I perish; though he frowns on me, I will not leave him, though he kills me, yet will I trust in him." Psalm 37:5, "Commit thy way unto the Lord, wait patiently for him, and he will bring it to pass."

3. The third degree of faith, is the faith of assurance. This is rare, and but few Christians have it. When the Spirit of God so shines in upon his own work in the soul, as to enable a Christian to speak triumphantly with the church, Song of Songs 2:16, "My beloved is mine, and I am his," or, with the apostle, 2 Cor. 5:1, "We know that when this earthly house is dissolved, we have an house in heaven."

Now poor complaining soul, if you do not have this faith of assurance, yet if you have the faith of adherence and recompence, your case is good. Assurance is not essential to justifying faith.

PART 3: Application

Is this so, that God in this way freely offers Jesus Christ to all that are willing to come to him? Then we shall make a fivefold use of this truth. We will make a use of:

I. Information.

II. Examination.

III. Exhortation.

IV. Direction.

V. Consolation.

The use of information shall be seen in six things. 1. If this is so, then this informs us of the desperate madness and folly of the greatest part of men in the world, who willfully reject Jesus Christ so freely offered in the Gospel. Should you see a poor maid begging her bread from door to door, clothed in nasty rags, and ready to perish with hunger and cold, and a great prince should offer his son in marriage to her, and this poor creature should refuse, and prefer her rags and shame before such an honorable state, would you not count this a stupid foolish creature? Why is this the case? Sinners by nature are in a woeful and miserable state, hanging over the very brink of hell, and ready every moment to drop into it, starving for lack of a Christ to save them; dead in sin, (Eph. 2:1-3). They are filthy, loathsome creatures, (Ezek. 16:1-11).

Now God freely offers Jesus Christ to poor undone miserable sinners, to be their Savior, to wash them from their filth. Ezekiel 36:25, "I will poor clean water upon you, and you shall be clean," *i.e.* "though you are black with sin, I'll make you white by washing you in my son's blood,[16] from all your filthiness, and from all your abominations will I cleanse you. I'll open your prison doors, and bring you into the glorious liberty of the sons of God. Accept of my son (God says) and with him you shall have pardon and life, grace and glory, and every good thing." And yet sinners will not come to Christ; here is the wonder, that men should prefer earth before heaven; a base lust before Christ; that a sick man should refuse health, a prisoner liberty, a condemned sinner pardon and life! And yet this is the case, we that are Christ's ambassadors come in the name of Christ, we pray you be ye reconciled to God, (2 Cor. 5:20). Come to Christ; but it is now as it was here in the parable, they

---

[16] Aspergam vos aqua munda, id est, Sanguine Christi. Sanguis Christi est quasi aqua munda cujus — Aspersione mundantur Electi, à sordibus peccatorum. Asperguntur autem hac aqua, corda electorum per fidem, qua credunt Sanguinem Christi, pro ipsis effusum esse in crucae in remissione peccatorum. Piscator in locum.

make light of it, and go away, one to his farm, another to his merchandize. No, sometimes it is to abuse the servant for offering them Christ, and begging them to accept him. O! what stupendous madness is this! This is to be more brutish than the beasts that perish. Isa. 1:2-3, "Hear, O heavens, and give ear, O earth; for the Lord hath spoken; I have nourished and brought up children, and they have rebelled against me. The ox knoweth his owner, and the ass his master's crib; but Israel doth not know, my people do not understand."

Objection: perhaps some may be ready to say, they do not believe that people are so unwilling to come to Christ; are we not all Christians, and do we not believe Christ to be the Son of God, the Savior of the world? Is there anybody but are willing to have Christ, and salvation by him?

Answer: the greatest part of men and women in the world will not come to Christ, as the scripture testifies here in this parable; they were invited, but they would not come. And John 5:40, "You will not come to me that you might have life."

Question: But who are they that will not come to Christ? Answer: 1. Those who were never thoroughly humbled for sin, will never come to, or accept of Jesus

Christ. Luke 5:31-32, "The whole need not a physician; but those that are sick. I came not to call the righteous, but sinners to repentance." Look abroad, how few ever had any humbling work upon their hearts?

2. Such as know not what it is to come to Christ, to believe in him, can never come to him. Romans 10:14, "How shall they believe in him of whom they have not heard?" Now what gross ignorance abounds almost everywhere?

3. Such will never come to Christ as think to be saved by something in themselves; its mere necessity that drives persons to Christ. Now, many people, ask them how they hope to get to heaven? Their answer is, by their good works; they pray, and keep going to their church, wrong no one, *etc.* Like that young man in Matthew 19:16, "What good thing shall I do that I may have eternal life?" There is no getting to heaven by our own duties and graces. Rom. 3:20, "By the works of the law shall no flesh be justified in his sight."

4. Such as do not heartily approve of Christ's terms, but have secret grudges, and heart-quarrels against Christ. Matthew 11:6, "Blessed is he who shall not be offended in me." The Jews quarreled at everything Christ did or said, at his birth, sermons, *etc.* And is it not

so now with many people? How frequently do men quarrel with the word, as that which is too pure? Where the commands are too strict? The threatenings too severe? *etc.*

5. Such who although they are convinced it is their duty to come to Christ, to repent, believe, yet delay, procrastinate; such as are mentioned in Luke 9:59-61. Christ bids them follow him. They do not deny but it is their duty so to do, yet they would put it off until another time. One would go and bury his father; another bid them farewell at his house. But this is a duty that admits of no delay.

6. Some would have Christ to receive them, but not on his, but their own terms; they would have him as a Savior, but not as a Lord. In Matthew 19:21-22 the young man was willing to have heaven, but not on Christ's terms.

I leave the enlargement of these particulars to your thoughts at leisure.

In this way it is evident, that among the crowd of the world, there are but few that do truly come to, or believe in Christ. There are other inferences, but I omit them for brevity.

The Believer's Marriage with Christ

II. Use of Examination. If this is so, that God in this way, freely offers us Christ, to be our Savior, then let us examine, whether or not we ever did believe in Christ, come to him, and accept of him on Gospel-terms. All our comfort lies in having Christ. 1 John 5:12, "He which hath the Son, hath life; and he which hath not the son, hath not life." Therefore, I implore you to try your own hearts, whether you ever did come to Christ or not. You might ask, "But how may I come to know this?" Take these signs.

1. All who ever came to Christ, first saw their need of Christ, their undone and miserable state without Christ. "The whole need not a physician, but those who are sick," (Luke 5:31). See how it was with St. Paul, before, in, and after the time of his conversion, Rom. 7:9-10, "For I was alive without the law once," alive,[17] *i.e.* I was a proud conceited pharisee, thought myself a righteous person, and in my own opinion was in a happy and safe estate as to my soul. Or, as St. Augustine expresses it,[18] I seemed to myself to live. But when the commandment came, he had it before but he did not understand it; but now he understands the spiritual

---

[17] Vivus eram: nempe opinio mea. Pareus.
[18] Vivus mihi videbar. August. lib. 1. cap. 9. ad Bonif. Vitam sibi arrogaret, quum tamen esset mortuus. Calvin.

meaning of the law, that it *cursed* him. Now, has it been this way with you? Have you ever been awakened by the Spirit of God, to see your undone, sinful, miserable estate? But do not mistake me; I do not mean, that mere trouble for sin is a sufficient evidence of your coming to Christ. No, Cain and Judas were troubled for sin, but never came to Christ; but when your trouble for sin, it drives you to Christ, (Matthew 11:28).

2. Such as have ever come to Christ, and believed in him, have seen the glory, excellency, fullness and perfections that are in Christ. There is indeed all manner of glories in Christ, but a carnal eye does not see them; the eye of faith only discovers the excellencies that are in him. Song of Songs 5:4, the spouse had had a sight of the fullness of Christ; and therefore, her soul was in pursuit after him. Now have you seen Christ's excellency? (2 Cor. 3:18). It may be you have heard of Christ, you have read of Christ, but have you seen him by faith?

3. Those that did ever come to Christ, were drawn to him by the ministry of the word, Rom. 10:17, "Faith comes by hearing." 1 Cor. 1:21, "It pleased God by the foolishness of preaching to save them that believe."

Now examine, you think you have faith; how did you come by it? Did you always believe? That is a sign that you did never believe. But have you found the ministry of the word to be the power of God to your salvation? (Rom. 1:16). Examine yourselves in this.

4. All those who have ever yet come to Christ, have divorced all their old acquaintance; I mean sins, with which the sinner is as intimate, as a man with his friend, (Isaiah 28:15). The sinner is in league and covenant with his sins, (Titus 3:3). There is nothing sweeter to the sinners taste, (Job 20:12-14). But now when a sinner comes to Christ, he casts all his sins away; there is now an absolute breach between the sinner and his sins, and not only gross and scandalous, but hid and secret sins, he hates vain thoughts, (Psalm 119:113). He forsakes both the way of sin, and also the thoughts of sin, Isaiah 55:7, "The wicked forsakes his ways, and the unrighteous man his thoughts." Now examine, is it so with you?

5. Such account it a singular honor to be employed in the service of Christ. Eph. 3:8, "Unto me, who am less than the least of all saints, is this grace given; that I should preach among the gentiles the unsearchable riches of Christ." What an honor did David

count it to be but a door-keeper in the house of God? Now examine; do you indeed esteem it your great privilege, that you may come and hear the word preached, that you may pray, that you may sit down at the Lord's table? Are these things counted greater honors and privileges by you, than if you had the prince's ear?

6. Such who have ever come to Christ, count an interest in Christ, and relation to Christ their chiefest treasures. Christ is to them that pearl of great price, which they value more than ten thousand worlds. 1 Peter 2:9, "To you that believe, he is precious." Do you see an excellency in Christ? Do your souls above all things thirst for an interest in him, relation to him, likeness to him?

7. Anyone like this who came to Christ in opposition to a right manner, they take as much pains for heaven in a way of holiness and obedience, as if there were no Savior, no mediator, but heaven were to be gained by works; and yet after all, they live as entirely by faith on Christ, as if they never had performed one duty, or done one good work. This you may see in St. Paul; never any after conversion did more than he did, much in prayer, fastings, and sufferings for Christ; and yet

never any lived more by faith than he did. Phil. 3:8-9, "I count all things but loss, for the excellency of the knowledge of Christ Jesus my Lord: for whom I have suffered the loss of all things, and do count them but dung that I might win Christ. And be found in him, not having my own righteousness, which is of the law, but that which is through the faith of Christ, the righteousness which is of Christ by faith."

Now examine yourself in this; do you work out your salvation with fear and trembling? Do you give all diligence to make your calling and election sure? Do you labor to be holy in all manner of conversation, denying all ungodliness and worldly lusts, and living soberly, righteously and godly in this present evil world? Do you take up every duty in point of performance, but lay them down in point of dependence, living only by faith on Christ?

III. The use of exhortation, to persuade every one of us to come to Christ. It was the work of these servants in this parable to invite people to Christ. And it is my work this day to persuade you, to invite you to come to Christ; O! that I could tell what words to use to prevail with you to come! You are invited not only to the marriage of the Son of God, but to marry with the person of the Son; Christ is offered to you in that sweet relation of a spiritual husband. Come, my brethren, will you have Christ? Do you see your need of Christ? Do not your souls long for a sight of Jesus Christ? Come, if you are but willing, have but a spiritual thirst, you may come and be welcome. Christ does not expect you should bring any price in your hands, Isaiah 55:1, "Lo, every one that thirsteth, come ye to the waters, and he that hath no money; come ye, buy and eat, buy wine and milk without money, and without price." So also see Rev. 22:27. It may be that you are willing to have Christ a Savior, but you must have him a Lord also. Many like Christ to bring them to heaven; but they are not willing to part with their sins.

Now that I may prevail with you to come to Christ, I will endeavor to do these three things. First, show you the excellency of the person you are invited to marry with. Secondly, the advantages that you will gain by coming to Christ. Thirdly, the danger of not coming.

1. To invite you to come to Christ. Consider what an excellent person Christ is: had you but a sight of those incomparable glories that are in Christ, it would raise your hearts in admiration of him; and give birth in you earnest desires of acquaintance with him. In Song of

Songs 5:8, you have the churches sickness for a sight of Christ. In ver. 9. The daughters of Jerusalem wonder at her, "what is thy beloved, more than another's beloved?" This is the usual language of a carnal person. You talk of the beauty and glory of Christ: what is there in him more than in another? To this the spouse answers, verse 10, "My beloved is white and ruddy, the chiefest of ten thousand." White in respect of his divinity, being God blessed for ever; and ruddy in respect of his humanity. Verse 15, "He is altogether lovely." Search all the world, there is none to be found like Christ, beautiful in his divine nature, as God. Heb. 1:3, "Being the brightness of his Father's glory, the express image of his person." Beautiful as man, Psalm 45:2, "Thou art fairer than the children of men." Beautiful in his offices, of prophet, priest and king. Though a carnal eye sees nothing, yet faith discovers wonders in Christ, (Phil. 3:8-9). The spouse describes him *cappape*, Song of Songs 5:10-15. Verse 11, his head, *viz.* his spiritual headship over his church, (Col. 1:18). Nothing is in Christ but is beautiful; his very locks, eyes, cheeks, lips, hands, legs, *etc.* are all beautiful, (verses 11-15). Understand these epithets spiritually, and Christ will appear a glorious and excellent person. O! Christians, labor to see and know

Jesus Christ; if you did know him better, you would desire him more.

    Secondly, to provoke you to look out after an interest in Christ, consider what you shall gain by coming to Christ.

    1. If you will heartily come to and believe in Christ, you shall have redemption and deliverance from the power and guilt of sin, and the tyranny of Satan. Eph. 1:7, "In Christ we have redemption, through his blood, even the forgiveness of sins." He will make you free for the New Jerusalem, which is above. Romans 8:1-2, "There is therefore now no condemnation to those that are in Christ Jesus. The law of the Spirit of life in Christ hath made them free from the law of sin and death."

    2. Come to Christ, and all your temporal maladies shall be sanctified to you, and all your spiritual maladies shall be cured: your temporal maladies shall all be sanctified to you; such as sickness, poverty, disgrace, reproaches, *etc.* All shall work for your good, (Romans 8:28). And your spiritual maladies shall be cured, such as infirmities, backsliding, ignorance, hardness of heart, blindness of mind, *etc.* Hosea 14:4, "I will heal their backslidings, and love them freely." Ezekiel 36:25-27, "I will pour clean water upon you, and you shall be clean;

from all your filthiness and abomination will I cleanse you; a new heart also will I give you, and a new spirit will I put within you: I will put my fear into your hearts, and cause you to walk in my ways."

3. Come to Christ, and you shall stand related in the nearest, dearest, and sweetest relations to God and Christ; you shall be his sons and daughters. 1 John 3:1, "Behold what manner of love the father hath bestowed on us, that we should be called the sons of God." 2 Cor. 6:17-18, "Come out from amongst them, and be ye separated, saith the Lord, and touch no unclean thing; and I will receive you, and will be a father unto you, and ye shall be my sons and daughters, saith the Lord almighty." You shall be his peculiar treasure, 1 Peter 2:9, "A chosen generation, a royal priesthood, a holy nation, a peculiar people." Jesus Christ will be to you a friend, (Song of Songs 5:16). This is my friend, my husband, (Isaiah 54:5). He will be a brother, sister, and mother, (Mark 3:35).

4. Come to, and accept of Christ for your Lord and Savior, and you shall be fed with dainty fare, and shall wear glorious apparel. Isaiah 55:1-2, "You shall eat wine and milk, yea that which is good." Jesus Christ himself shall be your food, and his righteousness shall be

your apparel. Ezek. 16:10, "I clothed thee also with broidred work, and shod thee with badgers skin, and I girded thee about with fine linen, and covered thee with silk." Verse 11, "I decked thee also with ornaments, and I put bracelets upon thine hands, and a chain of gold about thy neck." (See verses 12-13). All signifies the beauty of a believer in Christ; this glorious apparel is Christ's righteousness imputed outwardly, and the heavenly graces of the Spirit, put on inwardly in the great work of sanctification.

In a word, come to Christ and you have all in having him; Christ is heir of all things, he has all who have him, who is all.

Now if either love or beauty, or any excellency will draw you; here is all in Christ. O! sirs, come to Christ, I implore you that you do not refuse such a Savior.

Thirdly, yet once more to prevail with you to come to Christ, consider what a hell of misery you willfully throw your souls into, by refusing to come to him; what became of these in the parable, that set light by the invitations to come. Verse 5, they made light of it, and went away, one to his farm, and another to his merchandise. Verse 7, when the king "heard thereof, he was wroth; and sent forth his armies, and destroyed those murderers, and burnt up their city." O! it is a dreadful, a fearful case to refuse Christ offered. Heb. 10:28-29, "He that despised Moses's law, died without mercy, under two or three witnesses: of how much sorer punishment, suppose ye shall be thought worthy, who hath trodden underfoot the Son of God," *etc.* Refuse Christ, and you perish without remedy for ever. O! think of hell. Who among you can dwell in eternal burnings? Refuse Christ, and you sink without remedy into the lowest hell.

And therefore, I implore you come to Christ. What is the matter that you are so dead, and cold to this offer; why are you so backward? Christ is willing to receive. Isa. 55:1, "Lo, every one that thirsteth, come."

IV. The use of direction. Question: But how may a poor sinner come to Christ? I must now be short. 1. If you desire to come to Christ, then labor to see your need of Christ, your undone state and condition without Christ. I have told you it is mere necessity that drives people to Christ, (Luke 5:31-32). You must be sick of sin; like those in Acts 2:37.

2. If you desire to come to Christ, then you must beg and desire to be drawn to him. Song of Songs 1:4,

"Draw me, we will run after thee." John 6:44, "No man can come to me, except the Father which sent me, draw him. Sin has so enfeebled our natures, that we have no strength nor ability to do any good. Romans 5:6, "When we were without strength, Christ died for the ungodly." If you would come to Christ, see your own weakness, see your need of the drawings of the Spirit, and beg for it.

3. If you desire to come to Christ, then sit under a rousing drawing ministry. Romans 10:17, "Faith comes by hearing." Mark by what means so many thousands have been brought to Christ, and it has been by the preaching of the Gospel, as abundantly appears in these scriptures, Acts 2:37-38; 16:14; Eph. 1:13; 1 Thess. 1:6. This is that very ordinance that God has appointed to gather in the elect to himself. 1 Cor. 1:21, "When the world by wisdom knew not God, it pleased God by the foolishness of preaching to save them that believe." And indeed, this is the reason why the devil and his instruments so much oppose the preaching of the Gospel. O! prize this ordinance and wait daily at wisdom's gates. Observe where the Gospel is purely preached. Shun such preachers who cover sin and flatter, and heal the wound slightly. Some preach up a few dead ceremonies, cry up *the church, the church;* but

they do not preach Jesus Christ, regeneration, sanctification, and salvation by the blood, death and imputation of the righteousness of Christ. God does not own such preachers; but mark, those ministers that preach Christ, and free-grace, not free-will, such preachers as cut to the quick, Acts 2:37, keep close to the duty of hearing the word preached. If you slight the ministry, you will never come to Christ. When you are to change your relation or habitation, be sure to choose and prefer ordinances for your souls; go live under a godly ministry; hear constantly. Now and then, or on a Lord's Day is *not enough*; but in the morning sow your seed, in the evening do not withhold your hand, for who knows which shall prosper, this or that?

Objection: What if ministers will not preach twice a day? Answer: Such as know the worth of their own and people's souls, will be instant in season, and out of season. O! if that Scripture were but written on a minister's hearts, it would make them vigilant for God, Ezekiel 3:17, and tremble for fear they should be found guilty of the blood of souls.

V. I promised you a fifth use of consolation, to show you the sweet, happy, blessed state such are in, who are in Christ; but I have already exceeded the bounds of a sermon, and therefore all I shall say is that of the apostle, which gives you an account of that happy, sweet, blessed condition every man and woman in the world are in, that are come to Christ, Romans 8:1, "There is therefore now no condemnation to them which are in Christ Jesus."

FINIS

The Postscript to the Reader

Never did God show greater love to the sons of men, than when he gave the Son of his love to die for the sins of men; yet too many give away their souls for nothing. And though they will not now fear for love in the day of grace, shall hereafter tremble for fear in the day of wrath, and know, when too late, how much prevention is better than confusion.

And you that will not now come to Christ, by saving faith in the day of his love, to receive him with his merits and mercies, to your eternal consolation, shall after be brought to him in the day of anger to your eternal damnation. Now to do the one, and to avoid the other, remember you are but a pilgrim and stranger here, and that the great and chief end of man, is to glorify God, and save his own soul. That you may do this, be admonished carefully to pursue, conscientiously to peruse, and constantly to practice what is contained in this pocket-companion of being married to Jesus Christ as his bride.

The author of this work was a faithful preacher of the Gospel of Jesus Christ. You can see his qualifications from his biography in the beginning. His point of importance in this sermon, in which are many sweet, sacred, and soul-saving truths contained, were delivered by the author in the parish-church of Potters Pury, in the county of Northampton.

May the wisdom of heaven be opened, and distill down such heavenly refreshing dews on these sweet and sacred truths, that they may make a deep impression on our hearts, and be seated and settled in our minds, and become fruitful in our lives, to the honor of God, the joy of the author, and to the present comfort, future and eternal happiness of the hearers.

To conclude, that you may by this know how to put off the old man, and to put on the new man Christ Jesus, and so be made partaker of the divine nature, and at last come to have the full fruition of him in glory, is the earnest desire and prayer of

Your friend and servant in the Lord,
J.N.
Now minister of the Gospel at Potters Pury, aforesaid.
Perlege, vive, vale.

Other Helpful Works Published by Puritan Publications

Infant Baptism God's Ordinance
by Michael Harrison (1640-1729)

There is no better succinct, concise, precise and exegetically irrefutable work on infant baptism than Harrison's work. It is not just about baptism – it's about infant inclusion in the covenant of grace. It's about church membership. Anti-paedobaptists are going to find it literally impossible to refute Harrison's line of thinking, and, Paedobaptists will find a treasure-trove of biblical data to refute Anti-Paedobaptism.

Christ's Righteousness Imputed, the Saint's Surest Plea for Eternal Life
by Michael Harrison (1640-1729)

Christian believers have a hard time explaining their understanding of justification through the imputed righteousness of Jesus Christ. Harrison aids the reader to take an important doctrine, and make it simple to understand. It is one of his best works, and extremely valuable to the church today.

Taking Hold of Eternal Life in Christ
by George Gifford (1547-1620)

Is holiness of life a necessary prerequisite for getting into heaven? Do you have the power as a Christian to overcome sin? What has Jesus Christ done in enabling you to live righteously according to his commandments? How do you successfully glorify Jesus Christ in your daily walk?

The Christian's Deliverance by Christ and the Nature of Practical Religion
by John Kettlewell (1653–1695)

This work on Practical Religion, which centers on the Gospel of Jesus Christ, was Kettlewell's first work ever published, and was eminently popular. It takes basic Christian doctrine and makes it exceptionally practical.

A Call to Delaying Sinners
by Thomas Doolittle (1632–1707)

This work really needs no introduction; it would be enough just letting Rev. Doolittle loose on your soul. It is a puritan gem. Puritan evangelism at its best!

Joseph's Resolve and the Unreasonableness of Sinning Against God
by C. Matthew McMahon

How much do you hate sin? Joseph was resolved to cast off all wickedness as he lived before the face of God. Do you?

www.ingramcontent.com/pod-product-compliance
Lightning Source LLC
LaVergne TN
LVHW051528070426
835507LV00023B/3361